CLEANTECH SELL: THE ESSENTIAL GUIDE TO SELLING RESOURCE EFFICIENT PRODUCTS IN THE B2B MARKET

TONY MCDONALD, B.S., M.B.A

Cleantechsell.com Publishing

Cleantech Sell: The Essential Guide To Selling Resource Efficient Products In The B2B Market

By Tony McDonald, B.S., M.B.A

Published by Cleantechsell.com

Arvada, CO

Copyright ©2018 by Tony McDonald

ISBN: 978-0-692-19852-0

Find out more at www.cleantechsell.com.

TABLE OF CONTENTS

PREFACE

This book was written for the people and companies who are bringing resource efficient products to market. I like the term resource efficient instead of energy efficient because cleantech covers more than just energy. Simple example: water. Water is a critical resource that must be husbanded carefully, but it doesn't quite fit under the term "energy efficiency". Hence, I will use resource efficient product throughout this book.

Your company could be a startup or an established firm that is new to the cleantech space. I have organized the book with sections that have the most important information that you will need to successfully launch your product. The topics are not in any sequential order, they are just the most important things of which I think you should be aware.

I don't make any comments respecting product or technology, I have just assumed that your product is resource efficient (energy, water, etc.). The examples used for quantifying the value proposition are for electric energy savings, but they can be just as easily used for identifying savings of other quantifiable and priced resources.

This is not a long book: what, you busy business builders have time for the War & Peace of commerce? No, I have packed this book with the knowledge you really need for that cleantech build and presented it in concise language with external resources. I have not tried to recreate a general business book, or a general sales book, or a reference work on detailed financial analysis – there are many excellent such works available and you have probably read some of them. This one presents specific information for a specific audience and I hope it is useful to you. All the best to you in bringing your product to market successfully!

CHAPTER 1
THERE IS NO SUCH THING AS CLEANTECH, THERE IS ONLY MONEY

Question: Why are you in the cleantech business? To make money? To save the planet? To serve your customers? All of the above?

I start from a simple premise as a salesperson and entrepreneur: no matter what you sell, you sell money. Or rather, you sell the hope of your prospect having more money than they did before they had your product. Does that bother you? If so, get over it. This book is about the B2B (business to business) sale. Businesses are generally financially rational actors. Not completely, but for the most part.

I base this premise on many years of selling resource efficient products to companies ranging from laundromats and auto repair shops to multi-national Fortune 500 firms. Money is what all these firms are buying. Many like the environmental benefits as part of the deal, but I have yet to see one buyer suck up a negative financial decision because of the environmental benefits that a product offered. Serious buyers are every bit as financially discriminating with a cleantech product as with any other product.

Being rational and generally growth-minded, business prospects understand and respond to a positive financial value proposition. They don't generally respond to soft minded appeals to environmental guilt trips. This is not to say that many corporations have not made environmental responsibility an important aspect of their businesses, for many have. They have done so either because they wanted to or out of enlightened self-interest as a reaction to public, interest group, and investor pressure.

What all this means for you is that you must prioritize the financial over the environmental, if that was ever a competing interest for you. You will sell on the financial value of your product with the environmental benefits as a nice side benefit. Think of the environmental benefits as a marketing strategy because they open a new vector into a target company, and a new message.

I am a skeptic about cleantech, and you should be too.

I mention these things right up front because I want to ground your thinking in business reality. I am a bit of a skeptic, some might even say a cynic, regarding the "cleantech" industry. My skepticism may not apply to you at all because you see business as I do – but with ten plus years in the industry, selling to the big and the small, helping new companies get off the ground, I have met a lot of starry-eyed do-gooders who want to save the planet with their gee-whiz new cleantech product. If that's you, I have bad news.

And the bad news is: nobody cares. Most of the people you will try to sell to love being green – just not the green you have in mind. The green they have in mind is money and if you want to be successful with resource efficient products, the first thing you need to do is to understand this reality. Yes, some customers might spend a little for a showcase "greenwash" project to show their environmental bona fides, but I have yet to see one spend serious money on a cleantech project that did not hit their internal return-on-investment (ROI) and payback period hurdles. And I don't mean just Fortune 500 companies – this applies to everyone, big and small, public and private.

Sadly, I have also seen many cleantech companies underperform and eventually go out of business. Cleantech got off to a big start in the 2000's with venture capital money rushing in and then many of the early companies did not survive, never mind provide exit multiples acceptable to their funders. After that the Silicon Valley crowd, at least, went cold on cleantech and back to funding the infinitely scalable apps, websites, tech, etc. that have been their staple.

But don't despair! Within these covers I will show you how to make the most of the product you have, and even how to use the environmental upside of your product as a marketing tool. If you want to change (or clean up) the world while your prospects lose money on your product, good luck. You can change the world, but you must do it with a product that makes financial sense for your customers.

The cleantech fallacy.

I chuckle about the whole notion of a "cleantech" industry. I have read about universities offering degree studies in "cleantech". Huh? Like a cleantech company is somehow different than any other company? When I was part of a team building a company with a patented, proprietary and very energy efficient product, we were out raising money. When investors came by our office I got the impression that they expected to find a parking lot full of Priuses. Well, this company being in the manufacturing business and being in Colorado, the parking lot was more typically full of pickup trucks with rifle racks and dead elk in the back!

And the reason is simple: because there is really no such thing as a "cleantech" company. If you walked in our plant you would find: managers, engineers, sales people, shipping clerks, admins, financial people, and manufacturing techs. Guess what you would find at the manufacturing business next door? Managers, engineers, sales people, shipping clerks, admins, financial people, and manufacturing techs. There is no difference.

So the businesses are the same. What is different? Any business that is competitive has to offer its customers something of differentiable value: typically better, cheaper, or faster. Cleantech companies and products cannot survive by offering the same or worse levels of service (productivity, efficiency, performance, etc.) and cost, all in the name of being more environmentally friendly. Nobody is buying that and assume that your prospects won't buy it either. The core premise of a good cleantech or resource efficient product is that it will do the same or better job than another product at a lower total lifecycle cost and with fewer negative environmental externalities.

But isn't that what every product is supposed to do? Do people buy new cars that are slower, less luxurious and use more fuel, and pay the same or more? Or can a tech company offer a new smartphone that is slower, bulkier and more expensive than last year's? Of course not! Calling a product "clean" does not give it a free pass. Customers expect more, and in the best case the cleantech company develops and offers products that meet or exceed the performance of competitive products while reducing negative externalities (typically pollutants) and save money. That is real innovation and real value added for society, and you should be very proud of your company if your products can provide it to the market.

The financial savings from your product may not be realized up front because a resource efficient product may well cost more than a standard product. However, it usually has to offer a lower total lifecycle cost, payback period and ROI. And understanding this harsh reality, addressing it, and building a persuasive case around it will give your resource efficient product and company its best shot.

Too Good To Be True Syndrome.

Oddly enough, if your product is really good you could have the opposite problem, the "Too Good To Be True Syndrome". I learned about this problem myself the hard way. Here is the story:

I had recently joined a struggling company that had a new, gee-whiz, energy efficient air-conditioning product. The thing worked great and really did offer dramatic energy savings. In the best possible applications, the product could genuinely save 80+ % of the energy a competitive standard unit would use. Fabulous, right? Even I can sell that!

I found a prospect that was ideal, like darn near perfect. They had a big facility where they did plastic injection molding, which gives off a lot of heat and takes a lot of air conditioning to keep the process and equipment working properly and the operators safe from heat stroke. I dug in and did a thorough energy analysis, pored through their energy bills, engaged our engineers on the proper sizing, and came back with a detailed analysis. The analysis showed our product could save around 90% of their existing energy bill and give them a 7-month payback on the investment in our equipment. Once the equipment was paid off, the prospect would be banking a half-million a year on energy savings for the next twenty years.

I prepared a beautiful proposal with all kinds of analysis, all of which I stand behind to this day. I believed then, and I do today, that they would get the savings and payback we offered. With those kinds of numbers, plus some added benefits in the form of improved indoor air quality and employee comfort they couldn't possibly say no. Right? Until they did. And shattered my naïve thinking.

Here is the truth: sometimes, Too Good To Be True is both true and too good to be believable. If you tell someone that you can save them half or more of their energy and expense, sometimes they just can't get their heads around it and get comfortable. They want it to be true, but their experience tells them that it just can't be true. And all the charts, graphs, and analysis in the world won't change their minds. And worse, your product may sound like the fabled 100 mile-per-gallon carburetor.

In retrospect the smarter play would have been to under promise and over deliver. If I had pitched a 30% energy save and a three-year payback, that would have sounded possible and they might have bit. Then when they saw their energy bills and realized that they did get a 90% energy save they would have been our biggest fan. Live and learn.

So, enter this market with a skeptic's eye, because there is no magic in being a cleantech company. You will have to play by the same market rules and financial discipline as every other company. But being forewarned is being forearmed, and this book's goal is to show you how to be forearmed to win the battle to make your product a success.

Chapter Summary

- No matter your product, all you have to sell is money.
- You must express your product's value in monetary terms.
- Forget about cleantech, nobody cares.
- Avoid Too Good To Be True Syndrome, even if your product is that good

CHAPTER 2
PREMARKETING YOUR PRODUCT – GO TO THE PROS FIRST

Question: Who is your prospect and eventual customer? What are their needs and concerns? Are you sure you know who they are and what they care about?

Let me tell you a little story…about my first experience at a cleantech trade show. This was September of 2008 and the show was a big one at the San Jose Convention Center. Thousands of people attended, including both the public and tradespeople, distributors, and others in industries related to cleantech products. The hundreds of vendors there offered everything from bio-degradable caskets (bio-degradable like us, eh?) to high efficiency building envelope products to plumbing services.

I had recently joined a struggling cleantech company that had developed a compelling technology for a high efficiency air conditioning product. We had a great demonstration unit that showcased the product's technical capabilities. Hot air came in one end, dramatically cooler air came out of the other end, and all from a tiny box in the middle. It really was a fantastic demo unit and we were inundated with people stopping by to see our product. I mean literally, we were the belle of the ball and had more booth traffic than any other group that we saw. Three of us were in our booth and we talked non-stop ten hours a day for two days.

The guy in the booth next to us was pitching a retrofittable, selective flush unit for residential toilets. Interesting but not a show stopper and few people came by to see him. He was a nice guy and I felt bad for him. We couldn't stop talking and he couldn't get arrested, so he sat there and watched us give our pitch over and over.

Later on the second day the crowds abated a bit. The three of us were about talked out so we took a break and walked around the show to see what else was on offer. As it happened I was the first one back to our booth after about twenty minutes away and when I got there I noticed people at our booth looking at our demo unit – and the toilet guy from next door was giving them the pitch on our product! And he gave it well – he had heard it so many times, including all the questions that arose, that he quite competently handled the demo and the questions and passed out our cards. We had a good chuckle and I bought him a beer after the show closed. I hope he has prospered.

What I remember most distinctly about that show was not the overwhelming interest in our product from the general public, or even the toilet guy pitch-hitting for us. No, it was the curious but tepid response we got from people in the industry. The people we would look to be our first sale, the people who would take on our product, get behind it and pitch it to their trusted customers. People like electricians, HVAC contractors, energy efficiency retrofitters and the like.

They would come see our product, or I would approach their booth to talk to them about our fantastic new technology. They would take a careful look, ask some questions about the technology and how it worked, inquire where it had been installed and for how long and how it was performing.

Clearly these industry pros were interested in a new product and technology – but even though the trade show was in California, these pros were all from Missouri. The Show-Me state. They put little stock in our gushing enthusiasm for the product, or from the general public's obvious interest. Were they ready to sign up to rep the product? No, they held back their order books and said come see me after you have it installed for a couple of years.

Despite the lukewarm response from the industry people we left the show full of optimism from the public's reception. And with some cash to show for our trouble. We had driven out from Colorado in a truck and along with the small demo unit we brought along one of our full-sized production units, which fit in the bed. A rancher got so excited about the product that he offered us cash for the production unit, which we had no plans to sell. But we took him up on the sale and it paid for the trip. With the cash in hand I suggested a short stop in Reno on the way back but was overruled by my colleagues.

The response from the industry pros stayed under my skin. Why weren't they as enthusiastic as the public? This product was the proverbial new mousetrap, all patented and proprietary, and we had it. Its performance was unprecedented: how could they not see what we at the company knew so well, that this thing was poised to change the industry? The world! We were all going to get rich!

Word of Caution

If you are a cleantech entrepreneur you might have similar feelings. Certainly you have to be very optimistic about your prospects for success to start a new company, or introduce a new product to the market. But don't let your optimism get the best of you, be smart and start talking to the people in your industry very early on.

The tough lesson we learned was that many people who were less experienced, like the general public and even some industry people, were very excited about our product. But this wasn't the first rodeo for those industry pros. No, they saw shiny-new-object products and their promoters every week and they had learned, the hard way, not to jump too quickly on a new product until it had proven itself, preferably on someone else's facility and with someone else's customers.

When we later took our product to market full force I was quickly reminded of the reception in San Jose. No matter where we went we heard the same things: interest, yes, but lots of questions and few orders. The people we most needed to get our product into wide distribution were not going to blithely risk their businesses and customer relationships for our sake. Some would eventually do so after the product had been proved out, but many never did. And why should they? They had successful businesses that had fed them and their families for many years. Their old standby products were widely accepted, and they knew how to sell and service them. What was the real upside for them to drop a successful product line and start selling ours?

These industry pros, like those in most industries, live and die by their customer relationships. They are very reluctant to bring something new to a trusted customer unless they are absolutely certain that the new thing will work and will not jeopardize their existing relationships. The experience and natural cautions of these pros are valuable for you because their objections tell you what you need to overcome to successfully launch your product in the market.

A little bit of general sales advice.

I am a big believer in pain as a selling tool. To sell you must understand pain and be able to recognize who is experiencing pain – and just as importantly, who is not experiencing pain. Let me give you an example.

I was pitching our high efficiency air conditioning product to a data center in southern California. This was a small, privately owned data center of the type that rents space for other company's servers. The data center houses the servers securely, provides connections to the internet, and keeps them at the proper operating temperature. That last part gets expensive: this data center had a monthly electric bill on the order of $100,000, half of which went to running the servers and the other half, *$50,000 a month*, on running their air conditioning.

Looking at this data center prospect for an entry point for first contact to sell a more resource efficient space cooling system might lead you to call up their facilities maintenance people. After all, the maintenance people source, purchase, and manage the cooling equipment and are responsible for maintaining the data center at the proper temperature.

But that would be a bad choice, and here is why: the maintenance people don't have the right pain points. To be sure they *have* pain points. They will get in trouble if the data center can't hold the temperatures agreed to with their server customers. They will have to do more work if their cooling equipment fails a lot and requires a lot of maintenance.

What they don't have is a utility bill pain point. Let's say you approach them with a new technology that will cut 75% of their utility bill, but this new technology is unproven in data center applications. Their biggest pain point is failure to keep their data center cool, and your new unproven technology incurs that risk. They are not sure how much risk, but for sure it's more than they have now. And the 75% electric bill savings? They don't care because they are not rewarded for saving money. What is the upside for them to the downside of taking on risk? Zero. To summarize their level of interest. Zero. Chances of making a sale to the facilities people? Zero.

However, there is someone with a utility bill pain point, i.e., the person paying the utility bill. Stroking that $100,000 a month check to the utility company is pain. If you tell that person that you can put $50,000 in their pocket *every month*, with a six-month payback on capital investment, and they know that $50,000 drops right to their own cashflow, you will have their attention. That person, be it the owner, and especially the owner, or someone else being evaluated on improving financial performance and cashflow, will be very interested in your product. That does not necessarily mean they will buy, but they will take a closer look and balance the risk with the reward.

Back to our industry pros.

The pain point analysis just discussed applies equally to the industry pros. You know that the industry's ultimate customers can reap real energy and cost savings from your product, and that they will be interested in your product. But the industry pros have different pain points. What upside do they gain if their customer saves 50% of their electric, gas, or water bill? Nothing. However, your new product can cause them pain if the pro takes it on and it either does not sell, or it sells and then fails. Either way the pro makes less money for more hassle. Trust me, you will encounter this problem with your distribution strategy.

Early on in your product development identify your distribution channels and the firms and people you will be dependent on to sell your product. Chat them up and start asking questions so that you can flush out their concerns and develop responses. Don't try to sell them, just ask questions. My own personal belief is that the most important skill in selling is LISTENING, and this is the time to shut your mouth and open your ears.

What to ask of industry pros:

Show them what you have.

What is their reaction? Can they sell this product? For how much? How many a year? To whom?

What resistance do they expect from their customers when asked about the product?

Would they rep your product? Why or why not? If no, dig for why not. They are telling you that your product can cause them pain and you must figure out what it is.

Do they perceive your product as having a unique value proposition? Is it different enough from other products to earn a place on their shelf, or in their efforts?

What do they expect as validation or proof that the product works as advertised?

Take what you learn from the industry pros and use it to hone your product, your business model and your pitch so when you later ask them to rep your product for real, you will be ready and you can answer their potential objections.

Chapter Summary

- Be very sure you know who your prospects and eventual customers are.
- Be even more sure you know what motivates them, and what does not.
- Find the people you will be dependent on to sell your product and get them on board early.
- Find the people with the right pain and sell to them.

CHAPTER 3
THE FIRST, MOST IMPORTANT THING YOU MUST UNDERSTAND

Question: Which of your prospects will value your product the most? Which of your prospects will value your product the least? Why would these groups view your product differently, and to whom would you rather sell?

The value that a resource efficient product brings to the market typically varies by the market segment, and you must have an acute understanding of where your product adds the most value. Let's call it the highest and best use of your product, and once you understand it your marketing efforts will be easy to prioritize. Here is an example:

Let's say your new product is a new and dramatically more efficient air conditioner. This product uses half the electric energy of standard air conditioners, but it costs twice as much to purchase and install. Let's break down the value proposition:

Variables: electric energy rate, annual hours of use, capital cost.

Now let's look at two different applications for the product:

A vacation home in Montana where the climate is cool and 300 hours of air conditioning per year are required.

A data center in Honolulu that requires 24x7x365 cooling to keep the servers running.

Now let's analyze the product in each location/application using the three variables and comparing the results to the performance of a standard product in the same location/application:

	Data Center Honolulu	Vacation Home Montana
Electric energy rate ($/kWh)	$0.20	$0.10
Annual hours of use	8,760	300
Capital cost over standard product	$10,000	$10,000
Hourly energy use (kW) of standard product	7	7
Energy used per year (kWh)	61,320	2,100
Total annual cost to operate	$12,264	$210
Hourly energy use (kW) of new product	3.5	3.5
Energy used per year (kWh)	30,660	1,050
Total annual cost to operate	$6,132	$105
Annual $ save	$6,132	$105
Simple payback period (years)	1.6	95.2

There are two primary differences in the applications: cost of electricity and annual hours of use. And as you can see, the differences between the standard product and the new product (yours) in annual cost to operate, annual cost savings and payback period are dramatic. In both these applications your new product uses half the energy of the standard product, but the financial results are much different. Its not that your product does not work well in the Montana house – it does – but because the electric power rate is lower and it is used much less often, the financial results are vastly different.

Note: While I have not included it in this analysis, there may be opportunities to impact the financial results if rebates, tax credits, or other third-party incentives are available, which they frequently are, and which are discussed in the chapter on Utilities. If the electric utility and state government of Montana decided that they wanted to encourage the replacement of all old air conditioners, they could offer rebates and tax credits that could make the purchase of your product essentially free or nearly so. Obviously, you would include this in your analysis.

Stupid question. Into which application would you rather be selling your new product? Obviously the one with the fastest payback. But I have seen resource efficiency product companies wasting their time trying to sell into tough application situations because they did not have a firm grasp on the value that their product brings to market and therefore which prospects would value it most.

So now the question for you: What are the highest and best uses of your product? You must analyze the potential applications for your product and rank order them based on payback period or ROI so that you are attacking the right prospects. This will be a spectrum of applications, per the example of our air conditioning product:

Application/location	Electric rate	Annual hours of use	Payback period	Priority
Data center Hawaii	High	High	Short (1-2 yrs.)	1
Manufacturing Sacramento	High	Medium	Short (1-2 yrs.)	1
Cannabis grow Denver	Medium	High	Short (1-2 yrs.)	1
Data center Atlanta	Medium	High	Short (1-2 yrs.)	1
House Honolulu	High	Medium	Medium (2-4 yrs.)	2
Retail facility Dallas	Medium	Medium	Medium (2-4 yrs.)	2
House Phoenix	Medium	Medium	Medium (2-4 yrs.)	2
Casino Las Vegas	Low	High	Medium (2-4 yrs.)	2
Vacation house Montana	Low	Low	Long (5+ yrs.)	3
Apartments Boston	Low	Low	Long (5+ yrs.)	3

Once you have a firm grasp on the priority of your potential applications you can make the best choices on which applications to pursue and use your marketing dollars and sales efforts wisely. Be smart.

Chapter Summary

- You must understand who of your prospects will value your product the most, and why.
- You must perform a detailed analysis of the value your product offers.

CHAPTER 4
PRIORITIZING PROSPECTS

Question: What is the shortest path to maximizing your sales? In the jungle of prospects out there, who should you spend your limited sales efforts to reach?

You want to sell as much of your product as possible at the lowest customer acquisition cost. But how to do so? One way to start is to understand and segment your prospects on those metrics. Here is one way:

Let's say your product is installed in facilities. Your product is a new, high efficiency (low thermal conductivity) window. Every building has windows, but different buildings have different sizes of windows. These windows reduce heating and cooling requirements (any source – gas, electric, wood stove, etc.) by 90%.

Your prospects exist on a sliding scale from best to worst. Here is how to classify and prioritize them.

Prospect Facilities.

Let's start with the nature of the prospect's facilities. In the table below are different prospects segmented by the type and number of facilities they own and manage:

Number of facilities	Many (thousands)	Many (thousands)	Some (tens-hundreds)	Some (tens-hundreds)	Few (1-10)
Diversity of facilities	All the same	All dissimilar	All the same	All dissimilar	All dissimilar
Example	Chain retail – many facilities, all the same	Government, large corporates. – many facilities but all different	Regional convenience store/fast food chain	Data center chain, small hospital groups	Single building owners
Sales leverage	High	High	Medium	Medium	Low
Prospect priority	Best	Good	Good	Ok	Worst

The best prospects have thousands of facilities that are exactly alike. These facilities only have one window size, so you can reduce the cost of the windows through economies of scale. Installation is also easier because the install crews won't have to adjust to different situations at each building.

On the other end of the spectrum is a single building. It can only use a few windows and the install crews must work from scratch and can't repeat their work to get economies of practice.

Sales leverage is the concept of selling the most product for the least selling effort. A high leverage prospect is one that can buy a great deal of your product with only one sales effort (not one call, but one overall effort). Imagine you were trying to sell to Walmart with their thousands of facilities. One sales effort could result in selling to all of their facilities. This is summarized as "sell once, sell many". By contrast the low leverage sale is a one-off sale to a single facility. No matter how much effort is put forth only one facility's worth can be sold.

Product value.

Now let's look at the attractiveness of your product for different prospects:

Product value in the prospect's facilities	High – big resource save (payback 1-2 years). Could be due to high resource costs.	Medium – some resource save (payback 3-5 years)	Low – not much resource save (payback 6 years +). Could be due to low resource costs.
Technical limitations on install	None – fast and inexpensive	Some – a few difficulties with installation	Many – prohibitively expensive to install
Customer price/payback sensitivity	Low – happy with 3 year payback, have cash to buy	Medium – expect 3 year or under payback	High – expect 2 year payback, tight on cash
Sustainability receptivity	High – prospect values sustainability at nearly any cost and payback, has sustainability goals that trump payback hurdles	Medium – prospect places some value on sustainability goals but won't compromise payback/ROI hurdles.	Low – payback is king. Prospect has no sustainability goals.
Prospect priority	High	Medium	Low

The best prospects get the best performance from your product, don't have any install problems, can live with the payback period of your product, and have cash to invest. The worst are just the opposite.

Now let's put together the facilities characteristics and the prospect characteristics to finalize our prioritization tool: See Appendix A.

The high leverage sale, in the top right quadrant, are your direct sales prospects, addressable by your sales force. The value of your product to them is high, and because they have many facilities their potential sales value to your company is high, thus they are worth the time, effort and expense to pursue with your own sales force.

The prospects in the top left quadrant gain high value from your product, but because each one can only buy a limited amount of product their value to your company is low. These prospects are best pursued by your leveraged sales force of external reps and distributors, which keeps the cost of customer acquisition low.

Geographic prioritization.

A further step in focusing your sales and marketing efforts is to understand if there is customer concentration in your product market. Many resource efficient products provide different savings depending on the geography, and hence climate conditions, of the facilities where they are installed. If not geography and climate, there may some other criteria apropos to your product.

Here is an example of geographic segmentation for an efficient air conditioning product. This grid divides up the southwest US into major metro areas and identifies the salient characteristics to analyze the most attractive geographic areas for sales efforts.

Location	Population	CDD	Energy cost ($/kWh)	Market Potential (000)	% Market Potential	Cumulative
CA Los Angeles	13,000,000	1506	0.2	3,915,600	30.7%	30.7%
AZ Phoenix	4,500,000	4557	0.1	2,050,650	16.1%	46.8%
CA San Bernardino	4,500,000	1501	0.2	1,350,900	10.6%	57.3%
CA Sacramento	3,000,000	1408	0.3	1,267,200	9.9%	67.3%
NV Las Vegas	2,000,000	3348	0.1	669,600	5.2%	72.5%
CA Central Valley	1,600,000	2200	0.15	528,000	4.1%	76.7%
CA Palm Springs	600,000	4287	0.2	514,440	4.0%	80.7%
CA San Diego	3,000,000	761	0.2	456,600	3.6%	84.3%
AZ Tucson	1,000,000	3180	0.1	318,000	2.5%	86.8%
CO Denver	3,500,000	777	0.1	271,950	2.1%	88.9%
UT North	2,000,000	1193	0.1	238,600	1.9%	90.8%
TX El Paso	1,000,000	2314	0.1	231,400	1.8%	92.6%
CA Bay area	4,500,000	142	0.3	191,700	1.5%	94.1%
TX Midland/Odessa	700,000	2260	0.1	158,200	1.2%	95.3%

WA Seattle	3,750,000	788	0.05	147,750	1.2%	96.5%
NM North	1,000,000	1348	0.1	134,800	1.1%	97.5%
OR Portland	2,300,000	1144	0.05	131,560	1.0%	98.6%
UT St. George	250,000	2710	0.1	67,750	0.5%	99.1%
ID Boise	500,000	890	0.1	44,500	.03%	99.4%
CO North	500,000	609	0.1	30,450	0.2%	99.7%
CO Grand Junction	200,000	1200	0.1	24,000	0.2%	99.9%
NV Reno	250,000	695	0.1	17,375	0.1%	100.0%
			Total	12,761,025	100.0%	

Metrics:

Population is as stated.

CDD is Cooling Degree Days, which is defined as a degree-day above the standard temperature of 75°F (24°C), used in estimating the energy requirements for air conditioning and refrigeration. The higher the CDD, the more annual cooling is required.

Energy cost ($/kWh) approximates the cost of electricity in the geographic area.

Market potential is an artificial number, mathematically the product of population times CDD times Energy Cost for each area.

% of market potential by location is the percentage of the total market potential in all of the geographic areas divided by the sum of all market potentials.

As you can see, the top 8 of 22 geographic areas contain over 80% of the market potential. The bottom line is that sales efforts for this type product are better spent in Phoenix than in Boise.

So putting together the geographic with the prospect and facilities analysis, you can prioritize where your sales efforts should be concentrated, and how you should attack each market (via direct or indirect methods).

Prospect prioritization is a strategic sales exercise that you must conduct to make the best use of your time and sales and marketing dollars. Thinking clearly about their value will guide you to make the right decisions for deployment of your assets.

Chapter Summary

- You must understand your product's value to your prospects.
- You must understand your prospect's value to your company.
- Only after you understand both of these metrics can you prioritize your sales and marketing efforts.

Chapter 5
Distribution Channels

Question: How will your product get to your end customer? Who will tell them about your product? What do you know about what motivates the people who can make your product succeed or fail in the market? What are your choices for moving your product to market?

As a manufacturer of a B2B (as opposed to a consumer product) resource efficient product you will likely go to market in one or both of two ways:

Direct to end user prospects who will buy, install and use your product. These are typically larger companies; multi-site, even multinational companies that have many facilities that can use your product.

Indirectly to the end user through intermediaries like manufacturer's reps, distributors, installer/contractors and the like.

Any company, large or small, wants to use its marketing and sales dollars most efficiently. The question is, how to do so? Faced with two channels, direct and indirect, the company has to decide how to maximize sales at minimum cost. Let's look at making the best of both channels.

Direct channel.

For the direct channel, this will usually mean having internal sales people, starting with the CEO, reaching out to, meeting with and pitching direct prospects. This is an expensive business. Sales people with the presence, savvy, and contacts to operate at the national accounts level, who can credibly interface with executives of large companies, do not come cheap. Certainly they will be six-figure players, and when they do sell they will be looking for substantial bonuses or commissions. A large accounts rep can cost an easy $200,000 all in (base, bonus, benefits). And then you have to fly them around to call on people. Keeping a rep on the road most of the year can run $50,000-$100,000.

Yes, that's expensive. But if they can bring in multi-million dollar sales on a regular basis they can easily pay for themselves. But if your company is early stage, such reps are a big commitment.

Indirect channel.

The indirect channel is also known as the leveraged sales model. It is leveraged because your company's efforts are multiplied through the distribution channel to reach far more prospects than one internal rep can by themselves. Here are a couple different models, and there may be more in your particular industry:

Your internal rep -> distributor -> installer -> prospect

Your internal rep -> manufacturer's rep firm -> installer -> prospect

And there can be many other parties and permutations. If your product must be designed (specified) in by an engineering firm, then either you or your manufacturer's rep (or both) will be calling on those engineers to familiarize them with your product.

When the leveraged sales model works, it's great. You can expand your reach dramatically at very little cost. Your distributor or manufacturer's rep will reach many more people than you can, and in geographies far from your office. And the main advantage they bring is that they have well-established relationships with the people in their area. When they walk in with your product in tow, they are greeted as a friend and trusted ally that has specialized knowledge that the engineer, installer, or prospect needs.

Indirect channel participants.

Now for the bad news. All the people and companies in your leveraged sales model, be they engineers, manufacturer's reps, installers, contractors, whatever, share similar characteristics. What characteristics are those? Here they are, and I have learned these lessons from considerable personal pain:

They don't care as much about your product and company as you do. Did you get that? No? Here it is again, louder: THEY DON'T CARE AS MUCH ABOUT YOUR PRODUCT AND COMPANY AS YOU DO! Accept, right now, that you cannot rely on anyone else to sell your product because outside parties are concerned first with their own survival, not yours. Other companies and people don't care about your gee-whiz new technology and product. All they care about is themselves and feeding their families. Does this behavior sound terrible? It isn't, it is utterly rational, and these firms should do nothing else. Accept that these firms and the people in them don't care about you, your product, your company or your family. They care about THEIR companies and families, and you can count on them to act accordingly.

They are all lazy, greedy and risk averse. And I don't mean to cast aspersion on them because I know many fine people in all of these businesses. But as you know I am a skeptic and I try to be as realistic as possible about human nature, and in recognizing that human nature you will be guided to make the best decisions for your company. If you could make $10,000 for one hour's work, or for one month's work, which would you choose? Obviously, you would do it in an hour if you could. Does that make you lazy and greedy? Ok, let's use a kinder term and call it rational behavior, and I personally plead guilty to those charges. Well, that is also how engineers, reps, distributors, installers, etc. view the world. All these parties, like everyone else, wants to make the most money with the least amount of time and effort. If you want to get these parties on your side, you must convince them they can do so with your product.

And another dimension of their rationality is their risk aversion. These firms are not in low dollar, B2C (business to consumer), transactional sales. They are in high-dollar, high-trust, long term relationship sales. If they are successful it has taken many years and sales to earn the trust of their customers, and this trust IS their business. Their customers only buy from them instead of their competitors because they have a good relationship. If the rep, etc. pitches a product that fails, their relationship with their customer is damaged, and with enough damage they go out of business. So, they are wisely risk averse and are cautious about taking chances on unproven products.

Let's look at a couple of these players in detail.

Manufacturer's rep firms. These tend to be small businesses composed of industry veterans who learned the technical aspects of the field at one of the large manufacturers, where they also likely learned sales skills. Rep firms are purely sales organizations that represent manufacturer's products in their local community, typically to specifying engineering firms or installer/contractors. Like all of the firms in the leveraged sales model they sell a variety of products called a line card. They only make money when they sell the products on that line card.

Say the rep firm carries 30 product lines. Here is the inside scoop, told to me by many such rep firms: the firm's line card is divided into three pieces:

The top 10% of the lines (that's three product lines!) constitute the bulk of their sales and profits/commissions. They will sell those lines all day, every day because they make the most money with the least effort.

The bottom 20% of the lines get zero attention. They will sell them if someone calls asking but otherwise they won't lift a finger to sell them. In the worst case the rep firm has taken on the line just to keep it out of a competitor's hands without any intention of selling it, or just because it might occasionally help them close a sale. Yes, that happens. You think you have an active rep in the market and they aren't doing a thing to sell your product.

The rest of the line card (70%) are products that they will push with some effort if the top products are not taking up their time.

Because of these realities, the job of a company using manufacturer's rep firms is to get your product as high up the line card as possible, where it will get the attention and effort of the rep firm's sales people. And remember, unless your product is selling like hotcakes in the market, at high prices and margins, you have essentially zero power with reps. You are at their mercy and you have to persuade them to push your product, hard. How do you do that, and what makes a line attractive to a rep firm?

Your product sells a lot of volume with good margins. First and foremost. Rep firms and their employees are self-interested (see the lazy and greedy discussion) and they will spend their time and effort where they can get the best return.

Your company supports the product and the rep through frequent visits to their office and by traveling with their sales people to meet with end customers and/or engineering firms, installers, etc.

Your company is willing to host (and pay for) training and familiarization sessions (lunch and learns, etc.) with the rep firm's end customers and/or engineering firms, installers, etc.

Your company is easy to deal with. Your people are pleasant, they return calls quickly, and they are knowledgeable.

You provide quality collateral material and web presence to support your product and reps.

You show up at industry trade shows and support your reps by hosting events for them and their customers.

You protect your rep's business interests by not selling around them because if you do they will always find out and it will destroy your relationship with them.

You protect your rep's reputation by standing firmly behind your product and doing the right thing when problems arise after a sale. No product is perfect, so problems inevitably arise, which is not unexpected and happens to every product. The difference is in how your company handles the problem. Do it well, step up and do the right thing, and problems will be overlooked. If you have to put someone on a plane at your expense, do it. Don't leave a rep hanging in the breeze in front of their customer with a problem they can't fix.

Finally, your product is easy to specify, if your product is of that nature. Reps and their customers can easily get technical information without having to call your company for things like sizing, technical files, capacities, budget pricing, etc.

Wouldn't you prefer to deal with a company that does all of these things? Of course, you are a human being and you want to be treated well in a good business relationship. So do manufacturer's rep firms.

Distributors/stocking distributors. These are brick and mortar companies with centralized distribution, distribution centers, and typically many retail locations (stores). Their stores stock many different items to serve their local trade customers. Think of a plumbing distributor. Plumbers don't run around with water heaters in their trucks. If a customer needs one, they go to the local distributor and pick one up. Small companies tend to like distributors because they stock inventory. That means they will buy product without a final sale customer order. That means cash flow for the small company.

Installers/contractors. These are the companies that actually install the product for an end customer. As a result, they will likely have the most contact with your end customer. Sometimes they will actually sell the product to an end user and sometimes they will just install the product after it has been specified by an engineering firm. Unfortunately, these companies are the farthest from your company and aside from training sessions have the least contact with you. Also, like the rep firms they represent a variety of products and yours will have to fight for its survival with the installer/contractors. See the discussion about the manufacturer's rep firms.

These firms range in size from one-man shops to near billion-dollar corporations, but most typically have five to twenty employees. Their business is nearly always local and like the rep firms they live and die on their relationships. I find that they are even more risk averse than the rep firms because they generally have a smaller number of important customers and losing the confidence of one of those customers can be very damaging to their businesses.

Unlike the rep firms, which are composed of salesmen who generally never see, handle, or inventory the products they sell, the installer/contractors are hands-on people who build and install things. Because they install the product they will generally be the people who service the product, so they must be trained and knowledgeable about your product. Training a large number of firms dispersed across a wide geography can be time-consuming and expensive. If your business requires you to do so, you may want to consider hosting regional training sessions (providing food is always welcome), or an online training facility (www.walkme.com has a good solution).

What these firms have in technical competence they sometimes lack in financial sophistication. You cannot generally rely on such firms to present a detailed payback and/or ROI analysis of your product's value proposition. The exception would be larger installer/contractors that also have a dedicated sales force. What to do? Help them as much as you can. Here are a few ways:

Provide collateral material that covers the financial aspects of your product's value proposition. If the installer/contractor can't explain it, at least you can give a detailed example that the prospect can read for themselves.

If there is a manufacturer's rep firm between your company and the installer/contractor, make sure the rep's salespeople can make a sophisticated presentation. This is generally well within the capabilities of the rep firm.

If all else fails, offer to get on a conference call with a prospect and the installer/contractor. The prospect will be impressed that they get to talk to a "factory rep".

In summary, don't forget that the manufacturer's rep firm, or distributor, or installer/contractor may genuinely want to help sell your product because it will help them make money. But when it comes down to it, what they really care about most is their business, not yours. They are really your first sale because if they don't buy what you are selling, they won't be effective selling it to others.

Chapter Summary

- Enumerate and study the various channels by which you can take your product to market.
- Understand the motivations and methods of the participants in the market.

CHAPTER 6
THE SUSTAINABILITY VECTOR, YOUR MARKETING SECRET PATH

Question: Your resource efficient product is differentiated in the market by its technical performance which helps its financial performance. How can you use that fact to get out of the usual sales channels and get to right decision makers faster?

I start from the premise that every business wants to improve its top line revenue, its bottom line profitability, its cash flow, and the resource efficiency of its balance sheet. Generally speaking I have found that if you have a product that can achieve some or all of the above, you can get an audience with prospects.

So the first stop with any public company will be to review their annual report. How are they doing financially? What are their corporate goals? What insight can you glean from the report that gives you insight into their concerns? If nothing else, it can be useful to read the report just so you can mention something from it when in a meeting to show your in-depth preparation.

But you aren't selling a new paper clip that is one hundredth of a penny less expensive than any other brand. No, you have a gee-whiz, patented, proprietary resource efficient product that will not only improve your prospect's financial performance, it will also help save the planet! And that gives you a marketing hook to get attention. Prospects are inundated with the latest and greatest stuff, and the bigger the company, the more vendors who knock on their door. Ever try to sell to Walmart? Yeah, get in line, because every seller knows that with their scale, Walmart can make one order and take a vendor from rags to riches overnight.

Any company with any interest in what is now called "sustainability" has not only demonstrated its enlightened thinking, it has opened up a whole new avenue for people like you to reach them. This is particularly true for the large, publicly reporting companies. Many companies worldwide now publish an annual sustainability report along with their financial reporting. The global consulting firm KPMG has reported that nearly 95% of the global largest 250 companies (G250) report on sustainability, while over 6,000 companies worldwide report as well. That is a large pool of prospects to attack.

Sustainability reporting.

There is even a standard for sustainability reporting. The Global Reporting Initiative (GRI) (www.globalreporting.org) is an international organization founded in 1997 that develops and publishes standards for sustainability reporting. At their website you will find, among other things, their published standards and the uploaded sustainability reports for many companies around the world. At the time of this writing, over 300 sustainability reports are linked on the GRI site.

If you are targeting a company of any substance for a direct sale approach you will of course include in your research their website. In addition to the other things you can learn, focus on any sustainability concerns or initiatives they convey. If they publish a sustainability report (also called a "corporate responsibility report" or an "environmental report"), download and read it, looking for areas where your product can help them reach their objectives.

Let's look at an example. Staples (www.staples.com) is a large office products retailer with hundreds of stores. Looking at their corporate responsibility report (available for download at their website) you can see that they focus on four primary areas: Environment, Community, Ethics, and Diversity & Inclusion. The last three are not places where a resource efficient product vendor can probably help, so let's look under Environment.

Here we find opportunity. Staples cites the following as areas of concern: Recycling Solutions, Reducing Operational Waste, Responsible Sourcing, Sustainable Products, and Energy Efficiency & Renewables. If your product addresses any of those areas, check them out. Likely, the Energy Efficiency & Renewables area will be of greatest interest to you. Let's check there.

Five initiatives are included here: Energy Star building participation, Cleaner Sources of Energy (Solar), Energy Reduction, Transportation Network, and Carbon Emissions.

Can you help Staples get more of their buildings Energy Star certified? Tell them exactly how you can help them increase that number.

Can you help Staples increase their use of cleaner sources of energy? Tell them about that new mini-wind generator you developed and how it can offset 500 kW of their power needs.

Can you help Staples decrease the energy intensity (kWh/square foot) of their facilities? Lots of opportunity here because they look at HVAC, variable-speed drives, lighting, demand control, motion control and other technologies. Quantify how your product will help them achieve a 10% reduction in energy intensity across their facilities. You have to put it in terms of your prospect's interests.

Can you help Staples improve the sustainability of their transportation network of vehicles? Another area ripe with opportunity. Can your product make their vehicles more efficient, or help them drive fewer miles to do the same deliveries? Tell them how, and by how much.

Finally, can you help Staples reduce their carbon emissions 50% by 2020 compared to their 2010 baseline? That is their stated goal. Show them how your product can help them reach this aggressive goal.

You must understand what your prospect is trying to accomplish and then demonstrate, quantitatively, how your product will them reach their goals. And almost every company that publishes a sustainability report will have one or more people tasked to help reach their goals. Find them. Call them. Meet with them and pitch what you have.

I was initially skeptical about corporate sustainability initiatives, suspecting that no company would put real effort into reaching such goals, especially if they cost money. At my very first meeting with the facilities executives of a Fortune 500 company I asked them right up front "I see that your company has sustainability goals. Are those meaningful or not?" Their answer was straightforward: "our bonuses are partially dependent on meeting these goals." I took their word for it and those executives and that company demonstrated to me that they were sincere in every way. That doesn't mean that every company will be, but I start by giving them the benefit of the doubt.

Here is another key question that you must ask at the earliest opportunity: what is the company's internal hurdle rate? In other words, what minimum financial metrics must an investment meet to be attractive? The most likely answer will be stated in years and months. "We won't consider anything with over a 3-year payback" is a typical response. For large corporates the number is usually 3 years, but I have seen it as low as 24 months. That is a tough hurdle for many products, but at least you know what you must do. If your product has a 4-year payback and you can't improve on it, move on to another company that can live with your product's performance. Or figure out how to piece together incentives, rebates, etc. to get under the hurdle.

A little more general sales advice.

Be mindful of the little things because sometimes they really count. There are several large office supply companies in the US and of course they are fierce competitors. At one stage I was selling to all of them and I was extremely careful when meeting with any of them that all the office products I used carried their label. Yes, that meant that I would use different pads of notepaper in my notebook, making sure that the pad prominently displayed the brand of the company I was visiting. Once I was making a presentation to one of these companies and I needed to have a presentation printed and bound. The company I was visiting offered these services, but I got into town too late to use one of their stores so I ended up getting the work done at a FedEx Office shop because they were open 24 hours. Did I walk into the meeting with the office supply company the next morning holding a bag with FedEx Office branding? Not on your life! The morning of the presentation I swung by a local store of the company I was visiting, bought some paper and got their branded bag, threw the paper out and stuffed the presentation in the branded bag. You can be sure that I made a show of removing my bound presentation from the branded bag so all the people in the meeting could see that I had patronized their services. After the meeting I was talking to one of the participants and she mentioned that the first thing their employees typically did when meeting with a salesperson was to see if they were thoughtless enough to show up at a meeting with their competitor's branded office supplies. A small thing perhaps, but one certain to blow up a meeting if overlooked.

Chapter Summary

- Corporate sustainability initiatives are your secret marketing channel. Use them.

- Dig into your prospect's sustainability initiatives and understand what they are trying to achieve.

- Align your product's benefits with your prospect's stated goals and show how your product can help the prospect reach their goals.

CHAPTER 7
ESTABLISHING YOUR CREDIBILITY

Question: If you show up at a prospect's door, will they believe your product claims? What can you do to prove your product's capabilities?

I f you are a newer company without an established track record, or a company with a new product that is outside your previous area, you are going to have to establish your product's credibility before anyone will buy it in any quantity. There are several ways to do this, and most of them are slow and painful. Here are some examples:

Reference accounts/customer testimonials. This one may take a while but for a new product it is a must-have. A reference account is a customer who has used your product for some period of time and has had success with the product and is happy with both the product and the customer service they have received. Furthermore, the customer must be willing to be a reference for your product to your other prospects. You must be careful that too many people don't call one reference account and burn them out. Get several. What you want is for them to be candid but mostly positive about their experience. That means they had to have a good experience, so make darn sure that a potential reference account is willing to talk to others and will say good things.

Customer testimonials can range all over the map, from great to awful. I had one that set the standard for great and if you can find one, they are worth their weight in gold. Here is how it went down:

A data center manager for a US government agency had heard about our technology and called us up out of the blue. Someone on our end told him we could not help him and to please go away. Six months later the guy calls back and fortunately I answer the phone. Yes, of course we can help him, how soon can we meet? I spend the next two years working with this data center manager and an outside engineer designing a fabulous and innovative cooling system for his facility that uses almost no energy, and what it did use was solar powered. It really was fantastic, and we had a big grand opening with the local congressman in attendance.

A few months after the center opened I was in the center manager's office and I asked him if we could do a case study on the project, and he was happy to oblige. Then he reaches in his drawer and pulls out a DVD with a three-minute video about the center and its innovative and new energy efficient cooling technology (mine). He had made it at his expense to show to his government colleagues and would I like to use it? Yes, thank you very much! It would have cost us thousands to make a video like that and he had done it himself. For years this guy would travel around the world speaking at conferences, touting how great our technology was. One customer like that is invaluable. Go make one for your product. And speaking of case studies…

Case studies. A case study is a brief write up about a particular application, and of course the fantastic results that were achieved by your product. Depending on the product, you may have to leave the product in place up to a year to validate results. A good case study includes the following:

Pictures of the product and the installation.

The name of the customer and the facility where the product is installed.

Background on the installation. What about the facility made it an attractive candidate for the installation? Describe the poor situation before your product was installed. What were the customer's goals for the situation and for your product?

Why your product was selected. Direct customer quotes are great here. "We chose System X because of its advanced technology and while it was a new product, we found the upside so compelling that we decided to take a chance."

The results/testimonial. Another great place for direct customer quotes about how well the product performed and how the customer is buying for all their other facilities. Quantitative results are called for: percent resource save achieved, payback period realized, reduced maintenance expenses incurred, etc.

Utility reviews. If your product can be rebated or promoted by an electric, gas, or water utility, see if they have a test program to vet new technologies. Many times utilities will pay for such tests and if you can get a favorable review with a written report, fantastic, because you can tout that report to others.

Awards. There are many organizations that make awards for technologies, products, and businesses, and the more awards your company and/or product can get, the better. Winning such awards won't necessarily sell your product, but especially at the early stages of market entry they can either win over a skeptical prospect or get you on the radar at a Fortune 500 company. Here are some examples:

Bloomberg NEF (https://about.bnef.com/new-energy-pioneers/). This group selects 10 companies worldwide annually that have breakthrough technologies.

Cleantech Group (https://www.cleantech.com/indexes/global-cleantech-100/awards/). Annual award to innovative clean technology companies.

CleanTech Alliance (https://www.cleantechalliance.org/cleantech-awards/). Annual awards in various categories.

Cleantech Open (https://www.cleantechopen.org/). Cleantech Open is an accelerator that runs an annual competition that provides mentorship, business plan review, and funding opportunities for small cleantech companies. Awards are made in a variety of categories. Competitions are conducted in regions (Northeast, Southeast, Midwest North, Midwest Central, South Central, Rocky Mountain, Pacific Northwest, Western), culminating in a national competition.

Popular Science What's New (https://www.popsci.com/tags/whats-new). A monthly roundup of new and interesting products.

R&D 100 Conference (https://www.rd100conference.com/). Awards for various technology developments.

Local industry groups.

California Energy Commission (http://www.energy.ca.gov/). A state organization advocating and supporting energy efficiency.

Colorado Cleantech Industries Association (https://coloradocleantech.com/). A private group that supports cleantech in the state, offers competitions and awards in several industry verticals.

Massachusetts Clean Energy Center (http://www.masscec.com/about-masscec). MassCEC is a state economic development agency that supports the cleantech industry.

Many states have such organizations, either public, private, or both. And of course the US government has the Department of Energy (www.doe.gov) and its subsidiaries.

M&V (measurement & verification) testing. This is a test of a product in an application over a period of time where the equipment is monitored by measuring equipment and the results tabulated. This type of test is best done by or with the involvement of a credible third party (government, utility, university, industry group, etc.) that can vouch for the results. Sometimes large corporations will sponsor such tests to validate a product that they are considering. If your product does well, these tests can be gold because a written, detailed, technical report is usually provided.

Customer pilot testing. Large companies (the kind that are at the top of your customer prioritization list because they have hundreds or thousands of facilities and can buy large amounts of your product) may express interest in your product but be hesitant to go with a large-scale implementation without validating for themselves that your product works as advertised. This will frequently result in a pilot test situation, which is good and bad. The good news is that the prospect did not say no altogether, they said prove to us that your product works as advertised. The prospect will generally pay for a test installation of your product, which will usually be an M&V test (see previous paragraph). The bad news is that if your product is subject to annual seasonality it can take a year to get results. Make the most of the test period by getting closer to the prospect's people by communicating regularly and developing the relationship.

Bake-offs. This is a head-to-head test of two or more competing products, possibly on the same facility, and is usually monitored for performance. I have been party to such tests, which no vendor likes because your slimy competitor could fiddle with your product to taint the results! A report on the test may be produced, hopefully by an honest broker that did the testing.

Government organizations. Various government organizations may be available in your industry to do testing of products. NREL (National Renewable Energy Laboratory, www.nrel.gov), in Golden, CO, does testing and development of many types of resource efficient products. The Federal Energy Management Program (FEMP, www.energy.gov/eere/femp) conducts tests of equipment with published reports for federal government users. These are highly credible tests.

US Military. The US military branches periodically look for resource efficient products and will pay for tests of such equipment. There is a risk: you may not be entitled to a report from their test. I had this happen to me. It was great to make a sale of the equipment for the test, but after the test was done we had no test report to show to others.

Universities. Some schools have programs to test equipment. Example: the WCEC (Western Cooling Efficiency Center, www.wcec.ucdavis.edu) is a joint program of the California Energy Commission and the University of California, Davis campus. Getting a favorable test result and report from such a source can bring a lot of credibility, and since such organizations usually have many facilities a nice sales opportunity could be uncovered as well.

These are all great credibility builders so take as many of them as you can get. No matter what form of credibility testing you undertake, get as much testing as possible and be sure to ask for and get a printed report by a credible third party. Having one of your company's cofounders tout how well the product works on their own building doesn't have the same gravitas.

Chapter Summary

- You must prove out your product's capabilities with third-party validation.

- You must prove out your company's capabilities with third-party testimonials.

- Line up your validations as quickly as possible because prospects will ask for them.

CHAPTER 8
WHERE THE SAVINGS WILL COME FROM: THE UTILITY BILL

Question: How will your prospect pay for your great new product? Can you show him how your product will be not only free to him, but provide positive cash flow?

As we discussed in the chapter about quantifying your value proposition, there can be many aspects of cost savings that contribute to reduced total lifecycle cost, but typically the biggest one is going to be the energy savings in either electricity or other service (gas, etc.). Because of this, you need to get smart about the costs that your prospect is charged on their utility bill. Sounds easy, eh? Not so fast. If you think this sounds easy, I am betting you have never really dug into a commercial customer's utility bill or the associated utility's tariff schedule.

For the purposes of our discussion I will focus on the electric charges, although a similar analysis will work for other utility costs.

The Utility Rate Schedule.

Utilities charge their customers based on rates identified in their tariffs, and these tariffs are mind-numbingly complex. The cynic in me says they are complex by design so customers won't really dig into them, but putting that aside let's look at an example.

Pacific Gas & Electric (PG&E) is the big utility that serves northern and central California. As of this writing, PG&E's electric tariff has not less than 101 different rate schedules! Check it out for yourself: www.pge.com/tariffs/index.page. What you will see is that different utility customers are charged according to different rate schedules depending on many factors, among them the type of business (agricultural, general use, residential, etc.).

Within the rate schedule for a particular type of customer (Appendix B) there are various charges. There can be many of them, but the most important for you are:

The energy rate charges ($/kWh used). This is the charge for the total amount of electricity (kWh) used during the billing period.

The time-of-use (TOU) charges (differing rates depending on when during the day the electricity is used). This typically means that electricity is more expensive during peak periods (12 pm – 6 pm), and least expensive during the middle of the night. You will have to look at your prospect's rate schedule to determine how many different rates apply during each 24 hour period. Usually it's just two but can be four or more.

The demand charges (a charge determined by the maximum instantaneous (kWh) demand occurring during the monthly billing period). This one is expensive and getting more so and you must understand it fully. For example, if the customer has some heavy machinery that is used *only once* during the billing period but that has a high electric draw, the demand charge can be half of the total bill!

California in particular has recently increased its demand charges dramatically.

And finally, the seasonal differences (typically winter or summer). The three primary charges (energy rate, time-of-use, and demand) can vary by time of year, with summer typically being more expensive.

Utility Bill Analysis.

There are two ways to estimate the electric energy savings that your product can provide: the easy way and the more accurate way.

The easy way: Get 12 months of your prospect's utility bills, add up the total dollars and kWh usage for the year, and divide the kWh into the dollars to get an average kWh rate. Example:

Total of 12 month's bills: $55,000.

Total of 12 month's kWh usage: 350,000 kWh.

Average kWh rate: $55,000/350,000 = $0.157/kWh.

Now, if your product can save the prospect 150,000 kWh throughout the year, you can show a dollar savings of 150,000 * $0.157 = $23,550.

The more accurate way: Again, start with 12 months of your prospect's utility bills. 12 months is the minimum you need because this time period will cover all of the seasonality of usage and billing rates. I typically lay all the charges out on a spreadsheet so I can see how the prospect is using electricity and the impact it has on the bill.

Next is to estimate the savings that your product can provide, and to do so as accurately as possible. Remembering the four major components of the utility bill (energy rate, time-of-use, demand, seasonal), what impact will your product have on these factors? Example: If your product can reduce electric usage during the peak period, then estimate by how much. If your product can reduce electricity usage during the summer, those kWh savings are more valuable than kWh saved during the winter. If your product can reduce or eliminate demand charges, homerun! By estimating the impact on all four major components of the utility bill you can look for ways to increase the potential savings your product can offer. And by presenting the detailed analysis to your prospects you can increase your credibility in their eyes by demonstrating your superior knowledge of the utility rate schedule, which confuses everyone, and no one wants to dig into.

But the real upside to doing the thorough analysis is to maximize the potential savings your product can offer, and in a believable way. If you can show your prospect, with a detailed analysis, how much your product will save them on their utility bill you have increased your likelihood of closing a sale.

Chapter Summary

- You need to get smart on validating the financial savings your product can provide.
- Understanding utility rate schedules in detail is a painful exercise, but you have to do it.

- Make sure you have identified all of the cost savings your product can provide.

CHAPTER 9
MONETIZING AND QUANTIFYING YOUR VALUE PROPOSITION

Question: How many ways does your product add value to your prospect? Can you dig deeper and find more ways?

Your product can bring value to your prospects in a variety of ways and to sell it you are going to have to enumerate those ways very clearly. You will have to create a proposal where you can demonstrate all that your product can do, so now it is time to think clearly and in depth about all the value your product can bring. There are three primary groupings: financial, environmental, and other.

I cannot tell you exactly what the components of each of these groupings will be for your product but below you will find a starting point.

Financial value proposition

I mentioned at the beginning of this book my conviction that B2B businesses only sell money, or the hope of more money in the future, to business customers. No matter how cool, unique, sustainable, etc., your product is, assume that your prospects will only buy your product because its value to the prospect can be and is expressed in financial terms.

To do that you must monetize the value of your product's performance. And that means identifying every possible, even remotely credible savings your product can provide. Here is a list of possibilities:

Operating expenses:

Electric energy savings (see utility bill discussion)

Natural gas savings (see utility bill discussion)

Water savings (see utility bill discussion)

Sewer charges savings (see utility bill discussion)

Any other priced resources savings

Installation cost savings

Maintenance and replacement cost savings

And don't forget to project the increased cost of all of the above costs in the future, which will enhance the present value of your savings.

Capital expenses:

Capital cost savings. If your product is less expensive to buy than a competitive product. Don't forget to price in any rebates, incentives, etc. It is more likely that your product will cost more than a less resource efficient product, but it might be less.

Differential capital cost offset and payback. This is an item easily overlooked but is very important. If you are proposing replacing existing equipment that still works, your cost savings must cover all of the capital cost of your equipment, which can stretch the payback period.

However, if the equipment has to be replaced anyway, then your product only has to cover the differential capital cost between your product and a less efficient competitor, which can shorten the payback period considerably even though your product is more expensive.

There are two scenarios:

Scenario 1. Let's say your prospect has legacy air compressors in a large factory. The existing air compressors do not require replacement, but your air compressor product costs much less to operate. Total cost to install your product is $1,000,000 and your product provides an annual cost savings of $125,000. The simple payback is 8 years.

	Total capital cost	Annual operating cost (energy, etc.)	Payback period of your product
Existing product	$0	$200,000	
Your product	$1,000,000	$75,000	
Annual operating cost save		$125,000	8 years

Scenario 2. Same factory, but this time the legacy air compressors are worn out and require replacement soon. The prospect is considering your product and a competitive but less efficient competitor. The difference here is that the prospect is going to have to replace the units anyway, so the difference in capital cost between your product and the

competitor is only $225,000, instead of the $1,000,000 in the previous scenario, and the payback period is thus much shorter.

	Total capital cost	Annual operating cost (energy, etc.)	Payback period of your product
Your product	$1,000,000	$75,000	
Competitive product	$775,000	$150,000	
Difference	$225,000	$75,000	3 years

Financing cost savings. If your product costs less than a competitive product, financing will obviously cost less. The accumulated interest charges can be represented in a cash flow model, as represented below.

Put it all in a model. Below you will find an example of a consolidated financial model for a resource efficient product vs. an existing system (Scenario 1 from above). Note that it includes capital (project) costs, energy costs, other priced resource costs (water in this case), and Operation & Maintenance costs.

See Appendix C.

Note that this model includes price inflation for all costs and provides a summary financial analysis.

Environmental value proposition.

The financial case for your product is first and foremost, but with that done you now get to tout the positive environmental impact that use of your product can provide. Again, you want to quantify this to as great an extent as possible, and most importantly *you want to tie to the prospect's sustainability goals*, if any and if you can find. From what I have seen looking through many corporate sustainability plans, the primary areas of concern are greenhouse gases (CO_2) and water. Let's look at each:

Greenhouse gas (primarily CO_2) from electricity production. This is a straightforward calculation of CO_2 emitted divided by kWh produced to get to lbs. CO_2/kWh. Raw data for this can be found from several sources:

US Energy Information Administration (EIA, www.eia.gov). Their website has a huge amount of information that can be very helpful to you so check it out. To get to the CO_2 and other air pollutants go to EIA's state by state page, www.eia.gov/electricity/state/.

US Environmental Protection Agency (EPA, www.epa.gov). EPA's eGrid database is very helpful (https://www.epa.gov/energy/emissions-generation-resource-integrated-database-egrid).

Carbonfund.org (https://carbonfund.org/how-we-calculate/).

Greenhouse gas (primarily CO_2) from burning fuels for heating. If your product can save on fuels directly used for heating, you should quantify the save as well. The US Energy Information Administration (EIA, www.eia.gov) has conversion tables available for this at www.eia.gov/environment/emissions/co2_vol_mass.php.

Water. Again, a simple calculation of gallons of water per kWh produced. Data is available from:

National Renewable Energy Laboratory (NREL, www.nrel.gov). NREL produced a very handy report, Consumptive Water Use For US Power Production, which you can find at: https://www.nrel.gov/docs/fy04osti/33905.pdf. This report shows water consumption per power generation by state.

Summary for presentation. Here is an example of an environmental section from a proposal to replace existing cooling equipment with a more resource efficient product:

"Installation of our units offers [PROSPECT] the opportunity to make a significant contribution to achieving its sustainability goals. By implementing this proposal, [PROSPECT] can make the following contributions to environmental responsibility:

	Current	Proposed	Save	Percentage Save
Electric usage				
kWh/yr	3,125,000	1,000,000	2,125,000	68%
$/yr ($0.15/kWh)	$468,750	$150,000	$318,750	68%
CO2 from electric generation (lb CO2/yr) (1)	4,187,500	1,340,000	2,847,500	68%
Potential CO2 savings (lb/yr)			**2,847,500**	

Cars taken off the road (2)			249	
PROSPECT CO2 reduction goal			**5,000,000**	
Percentage goal achieved with this proposal			56.9%	
Water usage savings				
Used at generation source (gal/yr) (3)	4,687,500	1,500,000	3,187,500	68%
Potential water usage savings (gal/yr)			3,187,500	
PROSPECT water usage reduction goal			**10,000,000**	
Percentage goal achieved with this proposal			31.9%	

Notes:

1. 1.34 lb. CO_2 created per kWh of electricity in this state (US EPA study)

2. Average car in US produces 11,450 lb. CO_2/yr (US EPA study)

3. Electric generation in this state uses 1.5 gal/kWh (NREL study)"

With a summary of this nature, your prospect has something concrete to show regarding sustainability, including and most importantly, its contributions to their stated goals.

Other value proposition

Be sure to identify other value adds that your product can provide for your customer, even if it is hard to put a number on them. Here a few that come to mind:

Indoor air quality. You may be able to quantify some measure of improvement: lower CO_2 levels, lower particulate matter, higher component of outside (fresh) air, etc. Can you tie this to better employee health, morale, lower absenteeism, etc.?

Facility indoor conditions. Is the facility better lit with your product? Or in some way more comfortable, or more productive? Perhaps fewer industrial accidents? Lower medical and liability costs, fewer lost days, greater output, higher quality?

Maintenance and replacement. This was mentioned in the Financial Value section. Sometimes this is easy to quantify (fewer light bulb changes, etc.) and sometimes not. Perhaps your new product reduces electric motor loading from 70% to 50%, thereby increasing the longevity of motors by five years. This pushes a big capital event five years out, which can be a considerable save.

Dig deep and figure out any possible value add that your product can provide and be sure to list it in your proposal, whether it can be quantified or not.

Chapter Summary

- Quantify your product's financial value to your prospect.

- Quantify your product's environmental value to your prospect.

- Quantify your product's other values to your prospect.

- The burden is on you to prove out the value your product can bring. Get creative and put yourself in the prospect's shoes.

CHAPTER 10
UTILITIES: HARNESSING THEM
TO HELP YOU SELL

Question: How well do you know what your prospect's power utility can do to help you sell your product? Did you even know they could or would?

U tilities can be a great boon to your product sales efforts through their rebate and product promotion activities. But before we go into the details of such programs, let's talk utilities in general.

When you think of a utility company you may think immediately of the company that provides electricity and gas to your house. For most of us, those are the largest utility companies, of which there are around 200 in the US and these serve most of the US population. But in total there are about 3,300 utility provides in the country, so around 3,100 of them are much smaller and serve smaller groups of customers.

The 200 large utilities are usually public, investor owned companies. Working with them is like working with any large bureaucracy. Think slow and bureaucratic. Their employees do not work with entrepreneurial urgency. Their paychecks and retirement are coming whether or not your product gets approved for their utility's rebate program, or for how much. You may be launching a company and desperately need to get your product into a rebate program so that it is more cost effective, so you can sell the product and feed your business. Utility employees don't care. Their kids won't go hungry if your product does not get approved. Keep that in mind when working with these firms. I don't mean to mischaracterize the employees of these utilities because I have dealt with many of them and they are generally nice, competent people. But their incentives are different from yours as an entrepreneur or salesperson.

The 3,100 smaller utilities take a variety of forms. They can be co-ops that are owned by a group of customers, they can be privately owned, and some are owned by municipalities. Some serve rural, agricultural communities. Many are non-profits. What I have noticed is that while their market reach is smaller than that of the big utilities, these small utilities sometimes offer bigger rebates. I have seen them provide rebates up to 70% of total installed cost. Those kinds of numbers can really move the needle for you.

How the utility can help you sell your product.

Your prospect's utility can help you in two primary ways: by providing rebates for equipment purchases and by promoting the sale of your products. Here is an example of such programs from Xcel Energy: www.xcelenergy.com/programs_and_rebates.

Rebates. These come in two forms: prescriptive and custom. For a list of utility, and other rebates, see: www.dsireusa.org, which maintains a comprehensive list of rebates and programs of many kinds throughout the US. Another source is IncentiFind (www.incentifind.com), which lists incentives and rebates, but works from a project perspective.

Prescriptive programs typically provide fixed amount rebates (say, $500) for the purchase and installation of certain products that the utility has pre-approved. To get your product into such a program you should contact the utility's rebate program. They will vet your product and decide if it belongs in their program, and if so, what rebate will apply. Then, whenever someone buys your product they can apply directly to the utility for a rebate.

Custom programs provide rebates of varying amounts based on the product to be installed, and these are more typical of commercial building installs. I have seen these vary in amount from 20% of the total installed cost up to 70% of total installed cost. But beware, most of these custom rebate programs require that the rebate be approved prior to the installation of the product receiving the rebate. Requirements for getting approval for the rebate vary but may include a detailed analysis of the energy savings to be achieved and that the product be vetted by the utility or some other authority. Contact the utility's rebate program for instructions on how to apply for their custom rebate program and do so with plenty of time to spare. Sometimes utilities subcontract out the work of rebate programs to a third party and you will be directed to work with them.

Promotion. Some utilities will even promote your product through their energy efficiency program. I have seen products listed on a utility's website, and of course that is of great promotional value to the manufacturer of that product. See this example from Southern California Edison: www.sce.com/wps/portal/home/residential/rebates-savings/rebates/. To get into such programs you have to apply to the utility and have your product vetted and approved.

Technology review. There is another way that a utility may be able to help you. Some utilities conduct ongoing research and product tests to find and support the development of new, energy efficient products. An example is the program run by the Sacramento Municipal Utility District (SMUD, www.smud.org), which runs a Technology Solutions program. Check it out at: www.smud.org/en/Business-Solutions-and-Rebates/Business-Rebates/Advanced-Tech-Solutions.

In such a program, a chosen technology is installed on a test facility and is monitored for energy use to determine if it performs as the manufacturer represented. The utility will typically pay to conduct the test, and best of all, will provide a report of the results. If the results are good, such a report can be absolute gold for a new technology trying to get noticed in the market, and it will help get the product in the utility's rebate and promotion programs. If the results are not good? Well, don't show anyone! Then go back and fix your product.

The biggest problem with utilities.

As we have seen utilities can help you in a variety of ways. From testing your product to promoting it to their customers, utilities can be a great boon for you. On the other hand, utility companies can move slowly due to their bureaucratic nature and size. But once you overcome the organizational inertia of a utility and get it moving in your direction, the utility can help you in a lot of ways and for a long time. So let's be clear that I am an unalloyed fan of utilities and what they can do for your company and of the help they have brought to my own personal sales efforts.

The biggest problem working with utilities is not their ponderous nature, it's how many of them there are. If your product can sell everywhere in the US, and if every utility would like your product, provide rebates for it, and ultimately promote it on their web site and through their activities, fantastic! Next question. How are you going to work with the 3,300 utility companies that cover the country?

Getting your product introduced to a utility, vetted by that utility, and even promoted by the utility takes time and effort. You have to meet with them, maybe they visit your business, tests are set up, test facilities are selected, products installed, M&V testing protocols are established, and results monitored. Then negotiations ensue over the rebate programs and amounts, etc. It's a lot of time, effort and expense to work with one utility company. Now multiply by 3,300 to cover the country. Yes, you could end up hiring a whole department to do nothing but work with utility companies.

Presuming that it will be impossible for your company to work with every utility company, the best you can do is to use the 80/20 rule and start at the top. Now we are back to the geographic prospect prioritization in Chapter 4. Which utility serves the most customers in the best geographic area for your product? Start with them. Then the next one down the list. Rinse, repeat.

Chapter Summary

- The good news is that utilities can help you sell your product in a variety of ways.
- The bad news is that you will have to work with the utility's large and slow bureaucracy to get the help they can offer.
- The worst news is that there are thousands of utility companies so you have to either hire a staff to work all of them or you pick and choose.

CHAPTER 11
PROJECT FINANCING AND CHANNEL ALTERNATIVES

Question: How many ways do you know to get your product to market? How many creative and interesting ways are there to help sell your product? What other companies can help you sell your product?

This chapter's title may be a bit confusing because the chapter covers two areas that overlap – financing and channels into the market. Let's start with the straightforward version of financing the purchase of your products.

Direct or indirect sale to cash buyer. Your product is sold to your prospect, either directly or through intermediaries like reps, distributors, contractors, etc. They pay cash or get payment terms. Easy.

Financed sale by buyer. The prospect buys your product either directly or indirectly and finances the purchase through its own sources. This could be a loan, lease, etc. You may or may not ever know that the sale was financed or leased.

Financed sale by seller. The prospect buys your product either directly or indirectly and finances the purchase through sources that you or one of your intermediaries provide. This could be a loan, lease, etc. There are many lenders and lessors who may be willing to work with your company to put together a financing package that you can present along with your product. The best-case scenario is to be able to go to a prospect with the following deal: $0 down payment, multi-year loan/lease terms, and immediate positive cash flow because your product's resource save is greater than the loan/lease payments. That's a deal you can sell!

PACE financing. Property Assessed Clean Energy (PACE) is a means of financing energy efficiency upgrades or renewable energy installations for buildings. If your product works in buildings, this could be a great source of financing for your products and a good marketing vector. PACE financing started out as a tool for residential energy upgrades but is now being used for commercial properties as well. Without getting into the legal weeds of how PACE financing works, the simple version is that a PACE loan is repaid by an annual assessment on the property tax bill, so the obligation stays with the property and is generally non-recourse to the borrower. This is a great tool that may be of real value to you depending on the nature of your product.

Not every state in the US offers PACE financing yet. At the time of this writing about 20 of the states allow commercial PACE loans. A good website to learn about PACE, how it works, and where it can be used is PACE Nation (www.pacenation.us). The US Department of Energy also has information about these programs (www.energy.gov/eere/slsc/property-assessed-clean-energy-programs).

PACE financing is a state government enabled, not administered program. There are a growing number of PACE lenders. Google "PACE financing" and you will be inundated with information. Here are a couple PACE lenders to start with:

PACE Equity (www.pace-equity.com)

Lever Energy Capital (www.leverenergycapital.com)

Here is something to keep in mind about PACE financers (like the two cited above): they are looking to place PACE loans. As part of their marketing to building owners they seek to make as many loans as possible, and for as large an amount as possible. If your product can contribute to improving the energy efficiency of a building, you should be developing relationships with these PACE lenders so that they know about your product and can recommend it to their customers. They can be a great marketing vector because they see many opportunities and can easily recommend your product to a project.

Channel alternatives.

The less straightforward versions are where distribution channels and financing merge and these can be very advantageous for your business. Here are some examples:

Energy Service Companies (ESCOs). ESCOs are companies that contract with public and private facilities owners to provide resource efficiency upgrades at no upfront cost. They typically do this using a performance-based contract model where they pay for resource efficiency upgrades and the customer pays them, with most of the payment coming from the energy save. Here are a couple places to learn more about ESCOs:

US Department of Energy: www.energy.gov/eere/femp/energy-service-companies-0.

National Association of Energy Service Companies: www.naesco.org/.

ESCOs serve government and large institutional customers. The good news is that their projects can be huge. Your objective with ESCO's is to develop relationships with them to get your product on their radar so they will specify it on their projects. This is not easy to do, especially not with a new product, because ESCOs are very technology risk averse. The reason is simple: when they enter into an agreement with their customer, they take the risk that a product will save energy as advertised and will last throughout the contract period, which can be 25 years. Expect to have a hard time getting them to specify your product, but if they do they could buy a lot.

The Department of Energy maintains a list of qualified ESCOs with contact information that you can find here: www.energy.gov/sites/prod/files/2018/08/f54/doe_ql.pdf. ESCO employees show up at large resource efficiency trade shows and conferences, like EnergyExchange, the Department of Energy's annual conference (www.energy.gov/eere/femp/energy-exchange).

Energy Services Agreement/Energy Performance Contracting (ESA/EPC). This is the mechanism that the ESCOs (and other) companies use to provide energy efficiency upgrades. There are other firms doing these types of structures. Here is an example: www.associatedrenewable.com/content/energy-services-agreement-esa. As with the ESCOs, you want to get your product on the radar of companies offering ESA/EPC so they will specify your equipment.

Engineering Service Companies (ESC). These firms vary in size and the range of services they provide but among other things they perform facilities management services at US military facilities. The form and scope of just what they do at a given military installation varies from place to place. Of most importance to you is that they staff Resource Energy Managers (REMs) at these installations.

The REMs and their companies are charged with improving resource usage at their assigned installation to meet the government's overall energy goals, so they are always looking for new products that can help them reach those goals. Selling in to these types of facilities can be difficult because of military security (you can't just walk on to a military installation and knock on a prospect's door), but they can buy a lot due to the large number of buildings on most installations. The place to start reaching out to these firms is with the companies themselves. Here are a couple firms active in the space:

Sain Engineering Associates (https://saineng.com/).

TetraTech (www.tetratech.com).

Other forms. A new type of energy services arrangement has been brought to market by a company called Sustainability Partners (www.sustainability.partners). They bill their model as "Sustainability as a Service", and their objective has been to bring a more innovative, "Silicon Valley" influenced model to the market. Their product is very innovative and differs from the typical ESA/EPC business model. Under the ESA model a customer signs a very lengthy 200+ page contract covering a 25 year period. Sustainability Partners' contract is very short and says they will install resource efficient products at their expense and if the customer does not like the results, that Sustainability Partners will remove the new equipment at their expense. The premise of both the ESA/EPC and Sustainability as a Service forms is energy savings that pay for energy upgrades, but Sustainability Partners is trying to make the model much simpler.

Chapter Summary

- Project financing ranges from the simple to the complex, and more options are opening regularly.

- As more resource efficient products enter the market, more ancillary financing and other players arise to help get these products into use.

- Keep your ear to the ground for new financing and distribution alternatives by attending trade shows, conferences, etc.

CHAPTER 12
SELLING TO THE US GOVERNMENT

Question: Do you know how they US government can help your product and company? Do you know how to sell to the government? Do you know that the government is always looking for resource efficient products?

Selling to the US Government is a detailed and complex subject for which there are many available resources online and elsewhere. There is an old adage "the government can be your biggest customer, but it will be your slowest customer". Or maybe I made that one up. For small companies, slow can mean death (or no cash flow, which is the same thing).

That said, the government has resource efficiency mandates and is generally always looking for and is open to more resource efficient products. The Energy Policy Act of 2005, with subsequent updates, gave the government mandates for its efficient use of energy in many areas, including buildings. In my own experience the government is quite sincere about improving its resource efficiency and is a great target prospect.

Here are few thoughts that may be of value if you are thinking of working with and selling to the federal government:

Your first stop must be the Small Business Administration website (www.sba.gov) that has links to many programs that could be of help.

The first thing to determine is whether your business qualifies for any special designations that will make it eligible for a variety of set aside contracting opportunities. Such designations/programs include:

Small business (below certain financial and other thresholds that vary from time to time).

Women-owned small business.

Service-disabled Veteran-owned small business program.

8(a) business development program (for businesses owned by economically or socially disadvantaged individuals).

All small mentor protégé program (for certain agricultural co-ops).

HUBZone program (for businesses located in historically underutilized business zones – this should be of high interest to you).

Natural Resource Sales Assistance program (to buy government resources – probably not of interest).

Gaining designation in any of these programs can make it easier to win sales to the government. The various ways are too complex to describe here but you should spend some time exploring what the SBA has to offer. SBA also offers counselors to help guide you through the system.

As a resource efficient product company, your second stop with the government should be the Department of Energy's (DOE) website (www.doe.gov). DOE has many initiatives in the energy space that you should at least peruse for value to your enterprise.

Also be sure to check out the Federal Energy Management Program (FEMP, www.energy.gov/eere/femp/federal-energy-management-program). FEMP's mandate is to help federal agencies meet their energy efficiency targets, and to do so they have many programs to help new technologies get established.

EnergyExchange Conference. Every year DOE sponsors a conference that is open to anyone, although it is attended primarily by people in the government and people who sell resource efficient products to the government. See the website (https://www.energy.gov/eere/femp/energy-exchange). This conference is a useful place to meet people in government and learn about the latest programs that DOE and FEMP are offering. And of course, the networking opportunities are fantastic.

The Government Services Administration (GSA, www.gsa.gov) is the US government's landlord and manages all its facilities. It is the largest landlord in the country, managing over 375 million square feet of space in over 9,600 buildings. GSA has an aggressive sustainability program and is always interested in new resource efficient products. Be sure to check it out at www.gsa.gov/governmentwide-initiatives/sustainability#/buildings.

GSA has a Proving Ground program that encourages and evaluates new technologies. Check it out at: www.gsa.gov/governmentwide-initiatives/sustainability/emerging-building-technologies.

US Postal Service. Another big government opportunity is the US Postal Service (USPS, www.usps.com). The USPS has over 30,000 facilities across the country and while most of them are retail post offices, they also have much larger facilities, like sorting plants that run to 500,000 square feet. And with their enormous fleet of delivery vehicles, they have vehicle maintenance facilities of substantial size. And of course a huge fleet of vehicles, if your company has something to offer in that area.

I sold a project to USPS some years ago and I found they had the best organized sustainability program I have yet seen. They had goals, plans, people assigned, and the money to get things done. It was quite impressive. Check out their current sustainability efforts at: https://facts.usps.com/sustainability/. Note from their sustainability page that their goal is to reduce energy used per square foot of building space by 25% by 2025. Maybe you can help.

Sales vectors into government opportunities. There are a variety of ways to sell your product to the government, a few of which are listed here. The first distinction is direct or indirect:

Direct sales. Selling directly to a government entity where you interface with government employees or contractors and the government buys from your company. This can be problematic (read:

slow) for a small company because you may have to get set up in various government payment systems. Among the ways to identify opportunities is:

FedBizOpps (https://www.fbo.gov/).

GSA (https://www.gsa.gov/acquisition/assistance-for-small-businesses/choose-how-to-sell-to-gsa).

Small Business Administration (https://www.sba.gov/federal-contracting/contracting-guide/how-win-contracts).

And there are consultants and other organizations that can help you sell to the government. Here is an example: https://www.federalcircles.com/. And there are any number of books, videos, guides, etc. online.

Indirect sales. Selling to a company or contractor that already has established government contacts, business and contracts is the fast way to get to government sales. By selling to one of these firms you can avoid direct contact with the government, which experience can range from cumbersome to intrusive. For example, to get listed on the GSA schedule (https://gsa.federalschedules.com/gsa-schedule/) a company has to submit to a review of its financial statements and performance, plus meet a variety of other criteria. Its much easier to sell to a company that already has government contracting in place.

Existing government contractors are not all large companies. On the high end are large ESCO firms like NORESCO (https://www.noresco.com/energy-services/en/us/), and on the small end they can be a local plumbing contractor for a military installation. But that small plumbing contractor has all the kinks worked out of his government contracting and likely has good contacts at the installation he serves. The biggest sale I personally made to the government went through just such a local contractor who was repping our product and who had many longstanding relationships at the military installation where I made the sale. The process for this sale is to find the contractors who have relationships on the installation and can get your product in front of the local government decision makers.

Chapter Summary

- The US government has many ways to help a resource efficient products company get off the ground.

- You should spend considerable time exploring what the government can do for your company and what resources it offers.

- The fastest path to selling to the government is likely through a company that is already doing business with the government, saving you the trouble of getting set up to sell directly to the government.

Chapter 13
Conclusion

Well, there you have it friends, and I hope that this work has been of some value to you. The cleantech industry is growing rapidly with many innovative firms popping up all the time. If you don't believe me, drop in to a CleanTech Open (www.cleantechopen.org) event sometime. Their competitions start in Spring and come to a head in the Fall, and if you go to one of their public events you will see some great new companies coming up.

Cleantech, when done right, is the best of creative entrepreneurship. The highest goal for those in the cleantech space should be to create technologies that reduce negative externalities (pollution among them) while raising the bar on performance. With products like that, cleantech *can* change the world.

Best wishes to you in your entrepreneurial journey from a fellow entrepreneur hacking through the same jungle.

Tony McDonald

Arvada, CO

September 2018

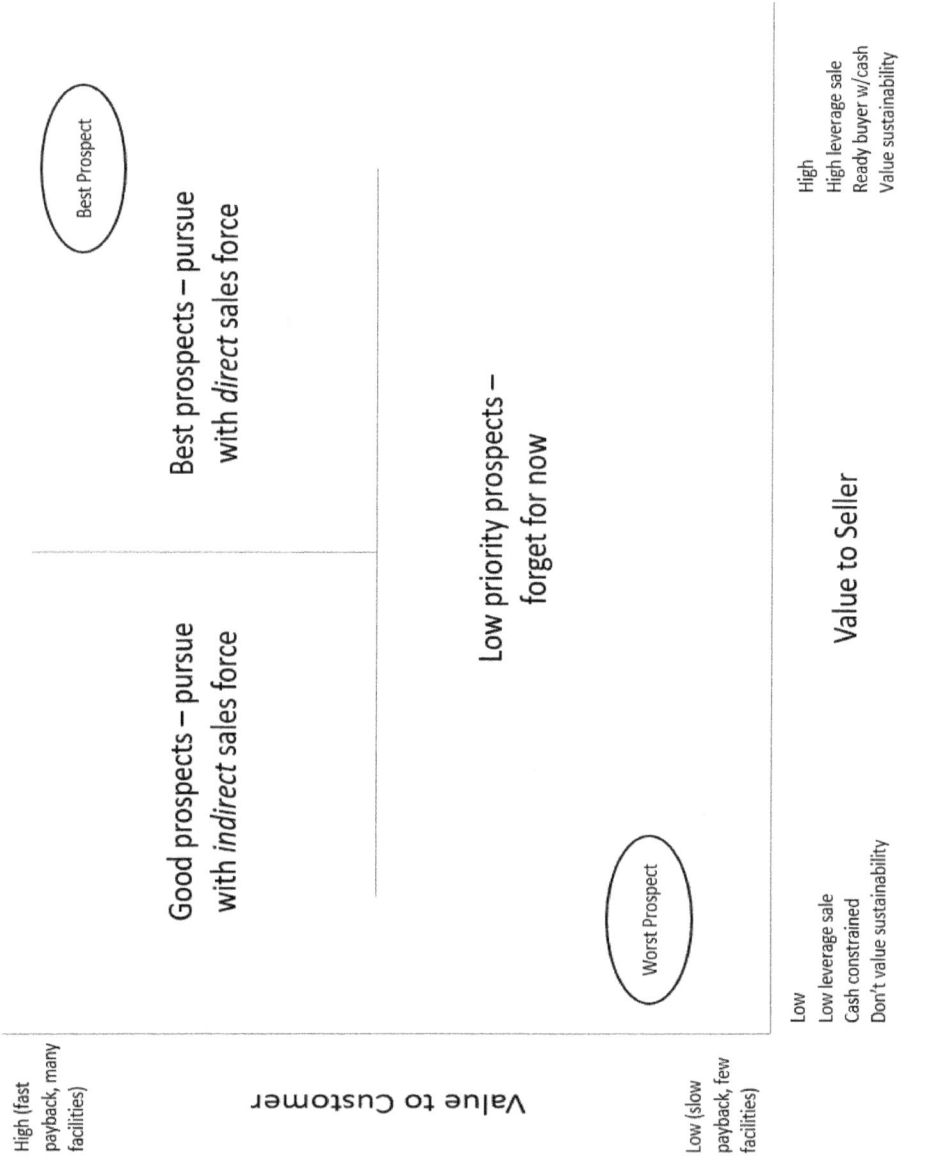

Value to Customer

High (fast payback, many facilities)

Low (slow payback, few facilities)

Value to Seller

Low
Low leverage sale
Cash constrained
Don't value sustainability

High
High leverage sale
Ready buyer w/cash
Value sustainability

Best Prospect

Worst Prospect

Best prospects – pursue with *direct* sales force

Good prospects – pursue with *indirect* sales force

Low priority prospects – forget for now

Appendix B
Utility Rate Schedule

ELECTRIC SCHEDULE A-10   Sheet 1
MEDIUM GENERAL DEMAND-METERED SERVICE

APPLICABILITY: Schedule A-10 is a demand metered rate schedule for general service customers. Schedule A-10 applies to single-phase and polyphase alternating-current service (for a description of these terms, see Section D of Rule 2*). This schedule is not available to residential or agricultural service for which a residential or agricultural schedule is applicable, except for single-phase and polyphase service in common areas in a multifamily complex (see Common-Area Accounts section).

Under Rate Schedule A-10, there is a limit on the demand (the number of kilowatts (kW)) the customer may require from the PG&E system. If the customer's demand exceeds 499 kW for three consecutive months, the customer's account will be transferred to Schedule E-19 or E-20.

Under Rate Schedule A-10, a bundled service customer with a maximum demand of 200 kW or greater for three consecutive months must have an interval data meter that can be read remotely by PG&E and pay the time-of-use (TOU) charges in accordance with the terms and conditions of this rate schedule.

Effective November 1, 2014, new customers establishing service on Schedule A-10 where a Smart Meter™ is already in place will be charged Schedule A-10 TOU rates.

The provisions of Schedule S—Standby Service Special Conditions 1 through 6 shall also apply to customers whose premises are regularly supplied in part (but not in whole) by electric energy from a nonutility source of supply. These customers will pay monthly reservation charges as specified under Section 1 of Schedule S, in addition to all applicable Schedule A-10 charges. Exemptions to standby charges are outlined in the Standby Applicability Section of this rate schedule.

Transfers Off of Schedule A-10 TOU: After being placed on this schedule due to the 200 kW or greater provisions of this schedule, customers who fail to exceed 199 kilowatts for 12 consecutive months may elect to stay on the time-of-use provisions of this schedule or elect another alternate time-of-use rate schedule.   (D)
(D)

Assignment of New Customers: If a customer is new and PG&E believes that the customer's maximum demand will be between 200 through 499 kilowatts and that the customer should not be served under an agricultural or residential rate schedule, PG&E will serve the customer's account under the provisions of time-of-use Rate Schedule A-10.

| APPLICABILITY | **Peak Day Pricing Default Rates:** Peak Day Pricing (PDP) rates provide customers the |
| (CONT'D): | opportunity to manage their electric costs by reducing load during high cost periods or |

Peak Day Pricing Default Rates: Peak Day Pricing (PDP) rates provide customers the opportunity to manage their electric costs by reducing load during high cost periods or shifting load from high cost periods to lower cost periods. Decision 10-02-032 ordered that beginning May 1, 2010, eligible large Commercial and Industrial (C&I) customers default to PDP rates. A customer is eligible for default when 1) it has at least twelve (12) billing months of hourly usage data available, and 2) it has measured demands equal to or exceeding 200 kW for three (3) consecutive months during the past 12 months. All eligible customers will be placed on PDP rates unless they opt-out to a TOU rate.

Decision 10-02-032, as modified by Decision 11-11-008, ordered that beginning November 1, 2014, eligible small and medium Commercial and Industrial (C&I) customers (those with demands that are not equal to or greater than 200kW for three consecutive months) default to PDP rates. A customer is eligible for default when it has at least twelve (12) billing months of hourly usage data available and two years of experience on TOU rates. All eligible customers will be placed on PDP rates unless they opt-out to a TOU rate. Customers with a SmartMeter™ system, or interval meter, installed that can be remotely read by PG&E may also voluntarily elect to enroll on PDP rates.

Bundled service customers are eligible for PDP. Direct Access (DA) and Customer Choice Aggregation (CCA) service customers are not eligible, including those customers on transitional bundled service (TBS). Customers on standby service (Schedule S), or on net-energy metering Schedules NEMFC, NEMBIO, NEMCCSF, or NEMA, are not eligible for PDP. In addition, master-metered customers are not eligible, except for commercial buildings with submetering as stated in PG&E Rule 1 and Rule 18. Non-residential SmartAC customers are eligible. Smart A/C customers may request PG&E to activate their A/C Cycling switch or Programmable Controllable Thermostat (PCT) when the customer is participating solely in a PDP event.

For additional details and program specifics, see the Peak Day Pricing Details section below.

Time-of-Use Rates: Decision 10-02-032, as modified by Decision 11-11-008, makes TOU rates mandatory beginning November 1, 2012, for small and medium C&I customers that have at least twelve (12) billing months of hourly usage data available.

The transition of eligible customers to mandatory TOU rates will occur once per year with the start of their billing cycle on or after November 1. Eligible customers will have at least 45 days notice prior to their planned transition date. During the 45-day period, customers will continue to take service on their non-TOU rate. Customers may elect any applicable TOU rate. However, if the customer taking service on this schedule has not made that choice at least five (5) days prior to the planned transition date, their service will be changed to the TOU version of this rate schedule on their transition date.

Qualifying customers with solar systems who meet the requirements in Rule 1 Definition of "Behind-the-Meter Solar TOU Period Grandfathering" and the terms of "Behind-the-Meter Solar TOU Period Grandfathering Eligibility Requirements" shall be permitted to maintain their legacy TOU rate periods, until the date ten years after their system received its permission to operate (but in no event beyond December 31, 2027 (for public schools) or July 31, 2027 (for all other qualifying). However, rates for those TOU rate periods will be updated with new rates as authorized in applicable PG&E rate proceedings and advice filings.

RATES: Standard Non-Time-of-Use Rate

Table A

TOTAL RATES

	Secondary Voltage	Primary Voltage	Transmission Voltage
Total Customer/Meter Charge Rates			
Customer Charge ($ per meter per day)	$4.59959	$4.59959	$4.59959
Optional Meter Data Access Charge ($ per meter per day)	$0.98563	$0.98563	$0.98563
Total Demand Rates ($ per kW)			
Summer	$19.85 (I)	$18.85 (I)	$13.00 (I)
Winter	$11.96 (I)	$12.26 (I)	$9.31 (I)
Total Energy Rates ($ per kWh)			
Summer	$0.17113 (I)	$0.15972 (I)	$0.12518 (I)
Winter	$0.13174 (I)	$0.12691 (I)	$0.10488 (I)

Total bundled service charges shown on customers' bills are unbundled according to the component rates shown below.

RATES: Standard Non-Time-of-Use Rates

Table A (Cont'd.)

UNBUNDLING OF TOTAL RATES

Customer/Meter Charge Rates: Customer and Meter charge rates provided in the Total Rate section above are assigned entirely to the unbundled distribution component.

Demand Rate by Components ($ per kW)	Secondary Voltage	Primary Voltage	Transmission Voltage
Generation:			
Summer	$5.41	$4.70	$3.69
Winter	$0.00	$0.00	$0.00
Distribution:**			
Summer	$6.27 (I)	$5.98 (I)	$1.14 (I)
Winter	$3.79 (I)	$4.09 (I)	$1.14 (I)
Transmission Maximum Demand*	$7.46	$7.46	$7.46
Reliability Services Maximum Demand*	$0.71	$0.71	$0.71
Energy Rate by Components ($ per kWh)			
Generation:			
Summer	$0.11614	$0.10620	$0.09638
Winter	$0.08916	$0.08282	$0.07608
Distribution:**			
Summer	$0.03121 (I)	$0.03006 (I)	$0.00584 (I)
Winter	$0.01880 (I)	$0.02063 (I)	$0.00584 (I)
Transmission Rate Adjustments* (all usage)	$0.00218	$0.00218	$0.00218
Public Purpose Programs (all usage)	$0.01342	$0.01310	$0.01260
Nuclear Decommissioning (all usage)	$0.00020	$0.00020	$0.00020
Competition Transition Charges (all usage)	$0.00099	$0.00099	$0.00099
Energy Cost Recovery Amount (all usage)	($0.00005)	($0.00005)	($0.00005)
DWR Bond (all usage)	$0.00549	$0.00549	$0.00549
New System Generation Charge (all usage)**	$0.00155	$0.00155	$0.00155
California Climate Credit (all usage)***	$0.00000	$0.00000	$0.00000

ELECTRIC SCHEDULE A-10
MEDIUM GENERAL DEMAND-METERED SERVICE

RATES: Time-of-Use Rates for Optional or Real-Time Metering Customers

Table B

TOTAL RATES

	Secondary Voltage	Primary Voltage	Transmission Voltage
Total Customer/Meter Charge Rates			
Customer Charge ($ per meter per day)	$4.59959	$4.59959	$4.59959
Optional Meter Data Access Charge ($ per meter per day)	$0.98563	$0.98563	$0.98563
Total Demand Rates ($ per kW)			
Summer	$19.85 (I)	$18.85 (I)	$13.00 (I)
Winter	$11.96 (I)	$12.26 (I)	$9.31 (I)
Total Energy Rates ($ per kWh)			
Peak Summer	$0.22501 (I)	$0.21165 (I)	$0.17270 (I)
Part-Peak Summer	$0.16988 (I)	$0.16109 (I)	$0.12583 (I)
Off-Peak Summer	$0.14181 (I)	$0.13446 (I)	$0.10052 (I)
Part-Peak Winter	$0.14153 (I)	$0.13796 (I)	$0.11404 (I)
Off-Peak Winter	$0.12446 (I)	$0.12208 (I)	$0.09946 (I)
PDP Rates (Consecutive Day and Four-Hour Event Option)*			
PDP Charges ($ per kWh)			
All Usage During PDP Event	$0.90	$0.90	$0.90
PDP Credits			
Demand ($ per kW)			
Maximum Summer	($3.61)	($3.14)	($2.46)
Energy ($ per kWh)			
Peak Summer	($0.00261)	($0.00380)	($0.00733)
Part-Peak Summer	($0.00261)	($0.00380)	($0.00733)
Off-Peak Summer	($0.00261)	($0.00380)	($0.00733)

*See PDP Details, section g, for corresponding reduction in PDP credits and charges if other option(s) elected.

RATES: Time-of-Use Rates for Optional or Real-Time Metering Customers
Table B (Cont'd.)

UNBUNDLING OF TOTAL RATES

<u>Customer/Meter Charge Rates</u>: Customer and Meter charge rates provided in the Total Rate section above are assigned entirely to the unbundled distribution component.

	Secondary Voltage	Primary Voltage	Transmission Voltage
Demand Rate by Components ($ per kW)			
Generation:			
Summer	$5.41	$4.70	$3.69
Winter	$0.00	$0.00	$0.00
Distribution**:			
Summer	$6.27 (I)	$5.98 (I)	$1.14 (I)
Winter	$3.79 (I)	$4.09 (I)	$1.14 (I)
Transmission Maximum Demand*	$7.46	$7.46	$7.46
Reliability Services Maximum Demand*	$0.71	$0.71	$0.71
Energy Rate by Components ($ per kWh)			
Generation:			
Peak Summer	$0.17002	$0.15813	$0.14390
Part-Peak Summer	$0.11489	$0.10757	$0.09703
Off-Peak Summer	$0.08682	$0.08094	$0.07172
Part-Peak Winter	$0.09895	$0.09387	$0.08524
Off-Peak Winter	$0.08188	$0.07799	$0.07066
Distribution**:			
Summer	$0.03121 (I)	$0.03006 (I)	$0.00584 (I)
Winter	$0.01880 (I)	$0.02063 (I)	$0.00584 (I)
Transmission Rate Adjustments* (all usage)	$0.00218	$0.00218	$0.00218
Public Purpose Programs (all usage)	$0.01342	$0.01310	$0.01260
Competition Transition Charge (all usage)	$0.00099	$0.00099	$0.00099
Energy Cost Recovery Amount (all usage)	($0.00005)	($0.00005)	($0.00005)
Nuclear Decommissioning (all usage)	$0.00020	$0.00020	$0.00020
DWR Bond (all usage)	$0.00549	$0.00549	$0.00549
New System Generation Charge (all usage)**	$0.00155	$0.00155	$0.00155
California Climate Credit (all usage)***	$0.00000	$0.00000	$0.00000

*   Transmission, Transmission Rate Adjustments, and Reliability Service charges are combined for presentation on customer bills.

**   Distribution and New System Generation Charges are combined for presentation on customer bills.

***   Only customers that qualify as Small Businesses – California Climate Credit under Rule 1 are eligible for the California Climate Credit.

APPENDIX C
FINANCIAL MODEL

PROJECT COSTS

Equipment	$ 150,000
Installation	50,000
Other costs	-
Sub-Total	$ 200,000
Less: Rebate or existing	(20,000)
TOTAL PROJECT COST	$ 180,000

FINANCING OPTIONS

Cash purchase ►

Monthly payment	$0
Annual payment	$0

TOTAL PROJECT COST $180,000

COST SAVINGS

	Annual Inflation	Year 1	Year 2	Year 3	Year 4	Year 5	Year 6	Year 7	Year 8	Year 9	Year 10
Energy Costs											
Existing system	5%	100,000	105,000	110,250	115,763	121,551	127,628	134,010	140,710	147,746	155,133
New system	5%	10,000	10,500	11,025	11,576	12,155	12,763	13,401	14,071	14,775	15,513
Energy Savings		90,000	94,500	99,225	104,186	109,396	114,865	120,609	126,639	132,971	139,620
Water Costs - additional											
Existing system	3%	0	0	0	0	0	0	0	0	0	0
New system	3%	2,628	2,759	2,897	3,042	3,194	3,354	3,522	3,698	3,883	4,077
Water additional cost		(2,628)	(2,759)	(2,897)	(3,042)	(3,194)	(3,354)	(3,522)	(3,698)	(3,883)	(4,077)
Operating & Maintenance Costs											
Existing system	3%	50,000	52,500	55,125	57,881	60,775	63,814	67,005	70,355	73,873	77,566
New system	3%	5,000	5,250	5,513	5,788	6,078	6,381	6,700	7,036	7,387	7,757
O&M Savings		45,000	47,250	49,613	52,093	54,698	57,433	60,304	63,320	66,485	69,810
TOTAL COST SAVINGS		132,372	138,991	145,940	153,237	160,899	168,944	177,391	186,261	195,574	205,352

CASH FLOW

	Year 0	Year 1	Year 2	Year 3	Year 4	Year 5	Year 6	Year 7	Year 8	Year 9	Year 10
Benefits (from Cost Savings above)		132,372	138,991	145,940	153,237	160,899	168,944	177,391	186,261	195,574	205,352
Costs (from Financing Options above)	(180,000)	0	0	0	0	0	0	0	0	0	0
Net Cash Flow - Annual	(180,000)	132,372	138,991	145,940	153,237	160,899	168,944	177,391	186,261	195,574	205,352
Net Cash Flow - Cumulative	(180,000)	(47,628)	91,363	237,303	390,540	551,439	720,383	897,774	1,084,035	1,279,608	1,484,961

SUMMARY

PAY BACK	Disc Rate	PV of 10 year cash flow
1.3 Years	10.00%	$984,823

Acknowledgements

To my dear friend and Army buddy Chip Armstrong, whose relentless optimism and unflagging inspiration have been a steady and welcome part of my life for many years. Here's to many more, friend. Airborne!

To my wonderful and long-suffering wife, Lisa. Thanks for staying the course and all my love.

ABOUT THE AUTHOR

Tony McDonald, BS, MBA is a successful businessman and sales leader. The wisdom, advice, and resources identified in Cleantech Sell is a compilation of the lessons learned in taking a cleantech company from zero sales, to dramatic growth, to winning awards and INC 600 recognition, and to eventual sale to a large strategic competitor. He also learned much as a mentor in the CleanTech Open, where one of his mentor companies won the competition and where he was Mentor of the Year in 2017 in the Rocky Mountain Region.

Tony earned an MBA from Harvard Business School and a BS degree in engineering from the US Military Academy at West Point. A former international consultant for KPMG and with many years in private equity, he has been a board member of both private and public companies and was proudly a Cavalry officer in the 10th US Cavalry (Buffalo Soldiers).

www.ingramcontent.com/pod-product-compliance
Lightning Source LLC
Chambersburg PA
CBHW071607200326
41519CB00021BB/6906